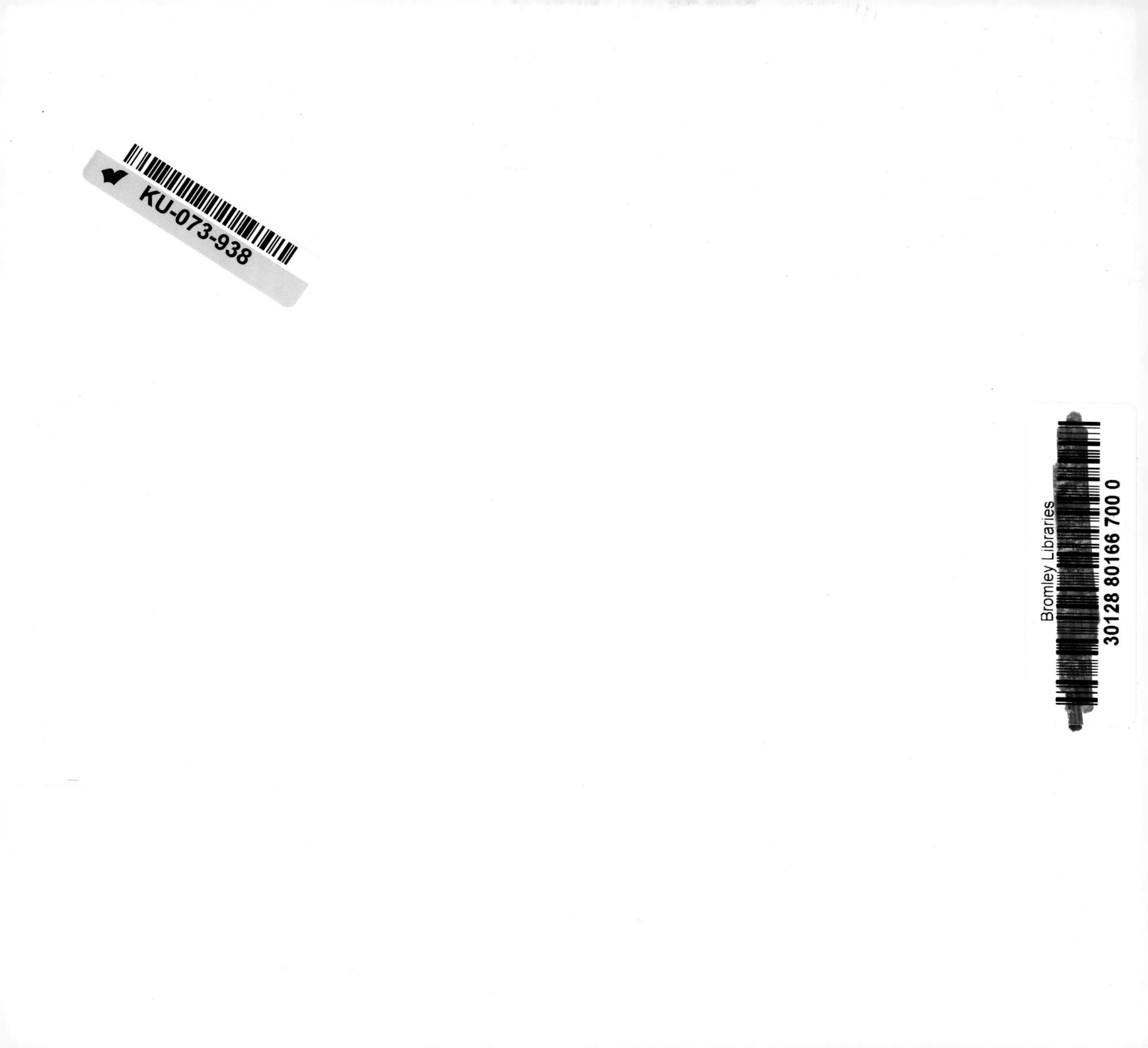
KU-073-938
Bromley Libraries
30128 80166 700 0

Let's read and talk about...

Family and Friends

Honor Head

FRANKLIN WATTS
LONDON • SYDNEY

Franklin Watts
338 Euston Road, London NW1 3BH

Franklin Watts Australia
Level 17/207 Kent St, Sydney, NSW 2000

This edition © Franklin Watts 2014

Created by Taglines Creative Ltd: www.taglinescreative.com
Author: Honor Head
Series designer: Hayley Cove
Editor: Jean Coppendale

Series literacy consultant: Kate Ruttle is a freelance literacy consultant and Literacy Co-ordinator, Special Needs Co-ordinator and Deputy Head at a primary school in Suffolk.

All rights reserved.

ISBN: 978 1 4451 3206 8
Dewey classification: 306.8'5
A CIP catalogue for this book is available from the British Library.

Picture credits
t=top b=bottom l=left r=right
Cover: Monkey Business Images/Shutterstock
Series icons: books, Osa; Jut; dddelli/Shutterstock; speech bubbles, Dic Liew/Shutterstock; hands, Zurijeta/Shutterstock
6 archana bhartia/Shutterstock; 7 Rob Marmion/Shutterstock; 8 Evangelos/Shutterstock; 9 GOGO Images/SuperStock; 10 Francisco Cruz/Purestock/SuperStock; 11t Tomasz Trojanowski/Shutterstock; 11b Margaret Smeaton/Shutterstock; 12 wavebreakmedia ltd/Shutterstock; 13 wavebreakmedia ltd/Shutterstock;14 Mandy Godbehear/Shutterstock; 15 wavebreakmedia ltd/Shutterstock; 16 Mandy Godbehear/Shutterstock; 17 michealjung/Shutterstock; 18 Monkey Business Images/Shutterstock; 19 Alexander Raths/Shutterstock; 20 Robert Crum/Shutterstock; 21 Bernad/Shutterstock; 22 J. Silver/SuperStock; 23 as cover; 24 Jacek Chabraszewski/ Shutterstock; 25 Dimitry Shironosov/Shutterstock; 26 Monkey Business Images/Shutterstock; 27 wavebreakmedia ltd/Shutterstock

Every attempt has been made to clear copyright on the photographs used in this book. Should there be any inadvertent omission please apply to the publisher for rectification.

Printed in China

Franklin Watts is a division of Hachette Children's Books, an Hachette UK company.
www.hachette.co.uk

Contents

What is a family?. . . **6**

Do all families have a mum and dad?. . . **8**

What about other relatives?. . . **10**

Why do some parents separate?. . . **12**

What is a step-family?. . . **14**

Should brothers and sisters be friends?. . . **16**

Who are foster and adoptive parents?. . . **18**

How should you feel when someone you love dies?. . . **20**

What makes a good friend?. . . **22**

Do best friends fall out?. . . **24**

What can be done about bullying?. . . **26**

Talk about . . . **28**

Glossary . . . **29**

Index and Activity sheets . . . **30**

Pages marked with ⬇ have a free downloadable activity sheet at www.franklinwatts/downloads. Find out more on page 30.

Words in **bold** are in the glossary on page 29.

What is a family?

A family is a group of two or more people who are related to each other.

TAKE ACTION Think of one thing you could do to help someone in your family and do it!

Who makes up a family?

Your **immediate family** are the people you live with, such as your parents and any brothers or sisters. Your **extended family** includes grandparents and other people who don't live with you but who are your **relations**.

Your mother and father and any brothers and sisters are your immediate family.

Does it matter who is in a family?

No, what is important is that the people who are in the family love and **respect** each other. Family members should care about and help each other. For example, many grandparents who have the time enjoy looking after their grandchildren after school.

Grandparents often help to look after their grandchildren.

Talk about

- **How do people in your family help each other?**
- **What could you do to help your immediate family?**

Why are some families different?

Every family is different. There are lots of reasons why we each have a different family. Also, families can change – a single parent might get married or two parents may decide to live apart.

Do all families have a mum and dad?

We all have birth parents but sometimes they don't live together.

Your birth mother is the mum who gave birth to you.

What are birth parents?

Birth parents are the mum and dad who are your **biological parents** – this means the mum and dad whose blood you share. Lots of children live with at least one of their birth parents but some children who have been **adopted** might never know their birth parents (see page 19).

Why do some families only have one parent?

If parents **separate** or **divorce**, the children might stay with either their mum or dad. Sometimes a child's mum has never lived with their dad. Sometimes one parent has to work away from the home for a long time. Maybe one parent has sadly died.

Talk about

- What are some of the reasons why parents may not live together?
- Does it matter if birth parents stay together?

Why do some kids live with two mums or two dads?

Sometimes men and women choose to have a **partner** who is the same **gender** as them. These **couples** often adopt children whose birth parents cannot look after them.

Two dads or two mums will care for you just as much as a mum and dad.

What about other relatives?

Your grandparents, aunts, uncles and cousins are all part of your extended family.

Why do some people have big families?

Some people have lots of relatives and others may have just a couple. In many parts of the world it is common for grandparents and other relatives to live with the family or close by.

Birthdays are a good time for families to get together and have fun.

What if you don't get on with some of your family?

There may be some members of your family with whom you don't think you have much in common, such as an older relative. Try to get to know them as they may have some interesting family stories to tell or an unusual hobby.

What can I do if a member of my family is horrid to me?

No one has the right to hurt you or make you do something you think is wrong. You should never be forced to keep a secret that makes you feel bad. If this happens, tell an adult you trust.

Talk about

- **What are the good things about having a big family and a small family?**
- **Who are your favourite family members and why?**

If someone in your family is hurting you tell an adult you trust, such as a teacher. Or call ChildLine, 0800 11 11.

The people at ChildLine will not tell anyone that you have called unless you want them to.

Why do some parents separate?

People separate or divorce for lots of reasons and this can be a sad time for all the family.

Whose fault is it when parents separate?

Sometimes people who live together feel they have grown apart or don't love each other any more. Whatever their reasons when parents separate, it is not the fault of the children. Parents who live apart will still love their children and want to be with them as much as possible.

You can still have a great time with your dad or mum, even if they don't live together any more.

What happens to the family when parents separate?

Usually the children live with one parent and have times when they see the other parent. Children can still visit all their grandparents and other family members to whom they are close. Even if your parents don't live together, your grandparents will still love you.

Whatever happens to your parents, your grandparents will always care about you and want to spend time with you.

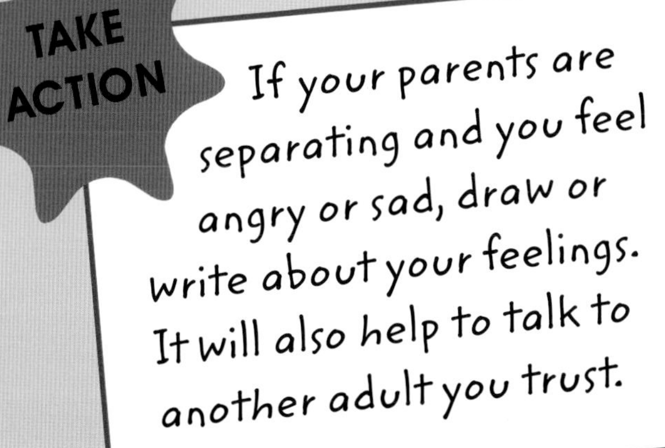

If your parents are separating and you feel angry or sad, draw or write about your feelings. It will also help to talk to another adult you trust.

When parents separate, do you have to take sides?

No, children can love both their parents even if they don't all live together. It's not fair for a parent to make a child take sides. If this happens, the child should talk to his or her parents and tell them how uncomfortable or confused this makes them feel.

- **Why do you think people separate or divorce?**
- **What do you think is the best way to cope with parents separating?**

What is a step-family?

A step-family is the new family a child might have when a parent has a new partner.

TAKE ACTION

If you have a problem at home, talk about it with a trusted family member, teacher or a friend. Don't keep your feelings bottled up.

Do step-families always get on?

It can take time to get used to a new step-mum or step-dad, and maybe new step-brothers and sisters as well. Some children may feel that the new family members are taking away their parent or invading their home.

Think of your step-brothers and step-sisters as new friends.

Can a step-parent tell you what to do?

A step-parent can tell you what to do and this can be hard. It might make you feel angry and confused. But remember they are trying to do their best to look after you properly.

A step-parent might be able to teach you something new.

Talk about

- **Why do you think it might be difficult to be part of a step-family?**
- **Why should you follow the rules of a new step-family?**

What should you call step-parents?

Some people call them mum or dad, others use their first names. If you feel really uncomfortable calling a step-parent 'mum' or 'dad', say so. Whatever you call them, you should treat each other with kindness and respect.

Should brothers and sisters be friends?

A brother or sister can be a great friend – but maybe not all the time!

Why do brothers and sisters argue?

Even close brothers and sisters disagree and argue – this is part of growing up. Having your own opinion about things is what makes you who you are. But it's important to understand that even someone close to you may not think or feel the same way you do.

Disagreeing with your brother or sister is fine, but listen to what they have to say.

TAKE ACTION

If you argue with your brother or sister, keep a note of what starts the argument. Is there a pattern? Talk to them about it.

Do brothers and sisters have to share everything?

Brothers and sisters should ask for permission to use what isn't theirs, not just take things. Sharing is an important part of being a brother or sister. As well as sharing your things, you should spend time together but also respect each other's privacy.

Brothers and sisters can help one another and enjoy being together.

- **What do you think are the best and worst things about having brothers or sisters?**
- **Do you think some brothers or sisters are spoilt? Why?**

What if you are an only child?

Being an only child means you may get more attention from your parents and have more space to yourself. But it can be lonely being an only child so friends are extra important.

Who are foster and adoptive parents?

Foster and adoptive parents are people who look after a child instead of their birth parents.

Why do children need foster parents?

Some parents love their children but cannot look after them properly for all sorts of reasons. Other parents may be hurting their children. When this happens the children are sometimes placed in a foster home.

Foster parents look after children until they find a permanent home.

Is fostering the same as adopting?

Foster parents look after children until they can go back home. Foster children sometimes move from one foster family to another. Usually foster children go back home when their birth parents are able to look after them. Some children are adopted after they have been fostered.

People who want to foster or adopt are asked lots of questions to see if they would make good parents.

Talk about

- **What do you think it would be like to live with foster parents?**
- **Why might a child be fostered or adopted?**

What happens when a child is adopted?

When a family adopts a child they promise to look after the child as if they were their own. The child takes on their surname, or family name, and becomes part of the family for ever.

How should you feel when someone you love dies?

The death of a loved one may make you feel very sad, angry, scared and confused.

Will you always miss the person who has died?

When someone you love dies you will miss them but that feeling will become less painful. You don't have to stop thinking about the person but remember how much the person loved you.

It helps to share your memories with someone else.

Is it okay to cry?

Whether you're a boy or a girl, crying is a good way to express how you feel when someone you love dies. It's okay to feel sad, angry and frightened. Try to talk to your family and friends about how you feel, or write or draw about it.

Do you always feel sad?

Over time you will feel less and less sad. Soon you'll be having fun again. This is okay and nothing to feel guilty about. You can remember the person you loved with a smile.

Talk about

- Why is it sad when someone dies?
- What are the best ways to remember loved ones who have died?

Photos will help you to remember all the happy times you had with the person who has died.

Read about What makes a good friend?

People who listen to our problems and care about us are our good friends.

Are all friends the same?

You can have lots of different types of friends. You might have friends who are also family, such as cousins. Some friends may go to the same school or club. You may have one or two best friends who are very special to you.

Some friends are very special; others you may only see at school.

Is it best to have lots of friends?

There is no rule about how many friends you should have. Some people like to have a lot of friends; others prefer to have just a few close ones. Close friends are the friends we care about and trust the most.

You can have a lot of friends but maybe only one or two who are close friends.

Talk about

- **What do you think makes a best friend?**
- **Why do you think you make a good friend?**
- **What could you do to be a better friend?**

How do you make friends if you are shy?

Making friends can be hard, especially if you're shy. Smile even if you're feeling scared. Ask people questions and listen to what they say – but don't be nosy. Ask them about their favourite music, films or football team rather than anything personal about their home.

Do best friends fall out?

Sometimes best friends fall out – remember friends don't have to agree about everything.

What if you fall out with your friends?

Even very best friends will disagree about something at some time so don't get too upset. Whatever happens try not to say anything nasty or rude to each other.

If you get angry with your friend, cool off and then talk about what made you angry.

What should I do if my friend asks me to do something bad?

If your friend wants you to do something bad, say no. Try to stop your friend from doing anything that might get them into trouble or hurt them. If your friend is doing something **illegal** or dangerous, you must tell an adult.

Friendships can change and you will meet lots of new people to be friends with.

Talk about

- Why do you think best friends might fall out?
- How can friends who fall out be friends again?
- When is it right to tell on a friend?

What if someone doesn't want to be my friend any more?

Sometimes friends find other people they would rather be with. It's okay to feel sad but try not to be angry. Try to talk to someone you trust about it. Join another group or take up another activity where you will meet different people.

What can be done about bullying?

Ignoring someone or spreading gossip about them is a type of bullying.

Bullying should always be stopped, at home and at school.

What is bullying?

Bullying is when someone hurts you or picks on you a lot. Bullying can be name calling, threatening someone, pushing, hitting or kicking or sending nasty emails or texts. Bullying can happen at home and at school.

What if my friend is being bullied?

Stand by your friend so that the bully knows your friend is not alone. Bullies usually like to pick on one person. Encourage your friend to tell a teacher or trusted adult about the bullying.

Should I join a gang?

It's good to be part of a group of friends who hang out together, but some gangs bully others and can be violent. Try to find out what a gang likes to do before you join. If someone in a gang tries to force you to join, tell an adult about it.

TAKE ACTION

If you are being bullied, keep a diary of every time you are bullied and what happens. Report it to a teacher, parent or **trusted adult.**

Talk about

- What do you think bullying is?
- Why do you think some people are bullies?
- What would you do if a friend asked you to join a gang?

Tell someone you trust if you're being bullied.

Talk about

✪ How many different types of families you can remember? How many people do you know who come from different types of families?

✪ Talk to your parents, teachers or grandparents about what families were like when they were young.

✪ Do you think families have changed a lot since your grandparents were married? Why do you think the changes are good, bad or neither?

✪ What are the best ways to deal with bullying and people who are being mean to you?

✪ How important are friends to you? How do you think friends help to make you happy?

✪ Why do some people find it difficult to make friends or be friendly?

Glossary

adopted when a child is chosen to be looked after by a non-related adult as their own

biological parents the mother and father who are related to a child by birth

couple the name for two people who live together as a married couple but they may not be married, or two people who have been together for a long time but live apart

divorce when a married couple decide to end their marriage legally. When a married person is divorced he or she can remarry

extended family all family members, not just the people you live with. An extended family includes grandparents, aunts, uncles, cousins, nephews and nieces

foster parents people who look after children until the child goes back to his or her family or is adopted

gender whether a person is male or female

illegal something that is against the law, such as stealing or taking drugs

immediate family the people you live with, such as your mother, father, sisters and brothers

memory box a box, bag or envelope where you keep special things that remind you of a person who has died. You can keep photographs, cards and letters in a memory box

partner the person someone lives with or is going out with

relations family members who are related to you by blood or through marriage

respect to be kind and to listen to what someone has to say, and to think about what they want as well

separate when two people who have been together as a couple decide they don't want to be together anymore

step-family if your mother or father remarries, the new family is your step-family

trusted adult an adult or older person who you know and trust, someone who can help you with a problem or difficult situation

Index

adopt 8, 9, 19, 29

biological parents 8, 29
birth parents 8, 9, 18, 19
brothers 6, 16
bullying 26

Childline 11

death 9, 20
disagreeing 16, 24
divorce 8, 9, 12, 29

extended family 6, 10, 29

falling out 16, 25
feelings 7, 11, 12, 13, 15, 17, 20, 21, 23, 24
foster parents 18, 19, 29

gangs 27
grandparents 6, 7, 10, 13

immediate family 6, 29

new friends 25

only child 17

privacy 17

relations 6, 10, 29
relatives 10
respect 7, 15, 17, 29

same gender parents 9
separation 12, 29
sharing 17
single parent 7
sisters 6, 16
special friends 22
step relations 14–15, 29

Activity sheets

The following spreads have accompanying worksheets, which are available to download for free at www.franklinwatts.co.uk.

What is a family? (pages 6–7)
Use this writing frame to explain who is in your family and write what you think about them.

What makes a good friend? (pages 22–23)
Answer the questions about friendship.

What can be done about bullying? (pages 26–27)
An anti-bullying poster.